Carlos the Chameleon

First published in 2018
by Jessica Kingsley Publishers
73 Collier Street
London N1 9BE, UK
and
400 Market Street, Suite 400
Philadelphia, PA 19106, USA

www.jkp.com

Library of Congress Cataloging in Publication Data
A CIP catalog record for this book is available from the Library of Congress

British Library Cataloguing in Publication Data
A CIP catalogue record for this book is available from the British Library

ISBN 978 1 78592 453 8
eISBN 978 1 78450 825 8

Printed and bound in China

Carlos the Chameleon

A Story to Help Empower Children to Be Themselves

ALICE REEVES

Illustrated by

PHOEBE KIRK

Part of the *Truth & Tails* series

Jessica Kingsley Publishers
London and Philadelphia

Carlos the Chameleon was a unique little creature. When he was being himself, he was a beautiful bright shade of green.

Carlos didn't have to be green all the time, though. He could change into any colour he wanted to, which meant he could fit in anywhere.

Some days, Carlos turned himself
pink and went splashing around in
the river with the flamingos.

Some days, he turned himself blue
and went jumping through the
canopy with the tree frogs.

Some days, when he was feeling tired, he covered himself in spots and sunbathed with the jaguars.

Carlos felt lucky to have lots of friends.

There were so many different
animals to have fun with, all he had
to do was change his colour.

He knew that if he was green,
then all the other animals wouldn't
want to be friends with him.

One day, when the sun was shining,
Carlos turned himself pink and went for
a swim in the river with the flamingos.

He was happily cooling his pink self down in the water when the tree frogs came jumping along the bank.

"Carlos, is that you?" asked Fernando the Frog. "Why are you pink? You're always blue when we go hopping through the trees."

As quick as a flash, Carlos leapt out of the water and turned himself blue.

"See?" said Carlos. "It's me!"

No sooner had Carlos turned from pink to blue, than the jaguars came stalking through the tall grass.

"Carlos, is that you?" asked Jade the Jaguar. "Why are you blue? You're always covered in spots when you relax with us in the sunshine."

Carlos panicked and turned
himself spotty so quickly that
it made him feel dizzy.

The commotion caught the flamingos'
attention and they came paddling over.

"What are you doing, Carlos?" asked Flora the Flamingo. "We just saw you turn from pink to blue to spotty.

"Why do you keep changing colour when you talk to different animals?"

Carlos felt embarrassed.

"I change colour because I want to be friends with all of you," he said.

"If I'm not the same colour as you, you won't want to be my friend."

He looked around at the flamingos
and the frogs and the jaguars,
who were staring at him with their
orange and black and golden eyes.

"Carlos, what colour are you?"
they all asked together.

"I'm green," said Carlos. He
let his spots fade away.

Before the other animals' eyes,
he turned his own bright and
beautiful shade of green.

He was greener
and brighter and
more beautiful
than all the trees
in the rainforest.

"Carlos!" exclaimed Flora the Flamingo. "You look so lovely when you're green!"

"Thank you," said Carlos, although he felt sad.

"What's the matter?" asked Fernando the Frog.

"Now that you know I'm green,
we can't do all the things we used
to do together," said Carlos.

"What do you mean?" asked Jade
the Jaguar. "Don't you want to
be our friend anymore?"

"Yes, very much!" Carlos exclaimed.
"But you won't want me around
if I'm not the same as you."

The animals looked at each other. They didn't understand what was wrong.

"Of course we want to be your friend, Carlos!" said Flora.

The flamingos nodded their long necks in agreement.

"It doesn't matter that you're green instead of blue," said Fernando.

The tree frogs croaked in agreement.

"We love being your friend because of who you are on the inside, not what you look like on the outside," said Jade.

The jaguars purred in agreement.

Carlos looked around at his friends.

They were all so different to each other, but that didn't matter.

He loved them all the same.

Besides, it was an awful lot of effort to keep changing colour every time he saw his friends.

The next time Carlos went swimming with the flamingos, he didn't turn himself pink.

He splashed about and shimmered
green in the tropical waters.

The next time Carlos went hopping through the trees with the frogs, he didn't turn himself blue. Although the frogs kept losing him in the leaves!

The next time Carlos lay in the sun
with the jaguars, he didn't turn himself
spotty. He relaxed and didn't worry
at all about what colour he was.

Carlos realised that he was happiest when he was being himself, which made all of his friends happy too.

Notes for Teachers and Parents

The following open questions can be asked to inspire discussion.

Circle time before reading

★ What does "fitting in" mean?

★ Have you ever done anything when you were with your friends to help you fit in?

★ Can you remember what it felt like doing something to try to fit in?

Older children

★ Have you ever changed your behaviour to be more like your friends?

★ Have you ever done something you wouldn't normally do to impress your friends?

Mid-reading questions

These questions can be raised midway through the story, when
Carlos's friends find out he changes colour.

★ Can anyone describe how they think Carlos is feeling and why?

★ What advice would you give Carlos?

★ What advice do you think the other animals will give him?

After reading

★ What does Carlos the Chameleon do to fit in?

★ Does trying to fit in work for Carlos? What makes you say that?

★ How do you think Carlos feels when he is changing colour to fit in?

★ How did he feel when he could just be himself?

★ What does Carlos teach us about fitting in?

★ What is it about you that makes you special
and amazing just the way you are?

Resources

Childline has a number of resources for children around dealing with different feelings and emotions, including building confidence and self-esteem: https://www.childline.org.uk/info-advice/ your-feelings/feelings-emotions

Acknowledgements

Thank you to everyone who has supported the *Truth & Tails* series from the beginning – without your help these books wouldn't have been possible.

Also in the *Truth & Tails* series

Molly the Mole
A Story to Help Children Build Self-Esteem

Molly is a mole with many friends, including a deer, a butterfly, and an owl. Sometimes Molly feels sad because she doesn't look the same as her friends, and feels very different to them. By helping each of them out with a task, Molly learns that her friends love her for the amazing qualities that are unique just to her.

Molly the Mole addresses the difference between the way we perceive ourselves and the way our friends and family perceive us. Molly learns the importance of being kind and patient with others, and that everyone is special in their own way.

Roxy the Raccoon

A Story to Help Children Learn about Disability and Inclusion

Roxy lives in the forest with her three best friends, who she loves to visit and play games with. Roxy is in a wheelchair, so sometimes it is harder for her to go to the same places and play the same games as the other animals.

Roxy and her friends realise that by making a few small changes and working together, they can make the forest a better place for everyone. Roxy teaches us that there are plenty of ways to be more inclusive of those who have a disability so that everyone can join in.

Vincent the Vixen

A Story to Help Children Learn about Gender Identity

Vincent is a boy fox who loves to play dress up with their brothers and sisters, but when they always choose to dress up as female characters, Vincent's siblings begin to wonder why.

Vincent comes to realise that they are actually a girl fox, and with the support of friends and family they transition to living as their true self. This is the story of one fox's journey to realising their gender identity and the importance of being who you are.